BREAKTHROUGH MARKSMANSHIP

BREAKTHROUGH MARKSMANSHIP

The Tools of
Practical Shooting

BEN STOEGER

Skyhorse Publishing

Skyhorse Publishing books may be purchased in bulk at special discounts for sales promotion, corporate gifts, fund-raising, or educational purposes. Special editions can also be created to specifications. For details, contact the Special Sales Department, Skyhorse Publishing, 307 West 36th Street, 11th Floor, New York, NY 10018 or info@skyhorsepublishing.com.

Skyhorse® and Skyhorse Publishing® are registered trademarks of Skyhorse Publishing, Inc.®, a Delaware corporation.

Visit our website at www.skyhorsepublishing.com.

Please follow our publisher Tony Lyons on Instagram @tonylyonsisuncertain

10 9 8 7 6 5 4 3 2 1

Library of Congress Cataloging-in-Publication Data is available on file.

Print ISBN: 978–1-5107–7936-5
eBook ISBN: 978–1-5107–7937-2

Cover design by David Ter-Avanesyan
Interior photos provided by Gaston Quindi Vallerga and Hwansik Kim
Illustrations by Jenny Cook and colorized by Brian Peterson

Printed in China

Contents

PART 1
INTRO

PREFACE:
THE TOOLS

"He wants to do the perfect job, not build better tools that work for all jobs . . ."

It was a smart thing to say, and the more I thought about it, it was a genius thing to say. I was discussing, as I sometimes do, a student of mine with my friend Gaston. Gaston is also a shooting instructor, competitor, and an international champion. He just so happens to live on a different continent and has a very different view of the world.

I described to Gaston my student, a man who was extremely motivated to do well and was willing to work hard, but would quit shooting halfway through a stage or a drill if it wasn't going well. Sometimes, he would stop shooting if he needed so much as a single makeup shot on a steel target or made some other minor mistake. I had been wrestling with this student's behavior for days. It didn't matter how much I yelled at him to continue shooting; he wouldn't listen. This student was such a perfectionist; if he made what he considered a mistake, he would stop and then reload his magazines and start the stage over.

This pattern was infuriating to me. I am fine with wanting to shoot an excellent run on a stage. I am fine with shooting the stage again and again in training to try and

accomplish this. I am very much **not** fine with building and reinforcing bad habits that will harm a shooter in the long run. Quitting in the middle of a stage isn't a pro-ductive habit; it is detrimental to progress. I described my frustration to Gaston, and it was evident we both understood this man's behavior as a problem. Gaston thought for a moment and then said:

Gaston Quindi Vallerga IPSC, IDPA, and USPSA Shooter and International Champion.

"He wants to do the perfect job, not build bet-ter tools that work for all jobs. IPSC is not predictable. The thing you should do is train to perfect your tools. Every stage is different, so you shouldn't worry too much about shooting every stage perfectly. Instead, you should develop your fundamentals, so you will do at least 'OK' in every situation. It isn't about being flawless; it is about being good, no matter the circumstance."

With that one paragraph, Gaston encapsulates precisely what this book is about. If you shoot USPSA, IPSC, IDPA, or any related shooting sport, then this book is designed to help you develop better tools. Not physical tools, but the technical tools you use when you shoot a match. Everyone wants to win. Everyone wants to shoot flawless, perfect stages. Not everyone understands that if your basic skills are improved, then as a well-rounded shooter, everything will get better. If you **are** the best, then you will tend to **do** the best.

The tools a shooter uses on each stage are the basic skills that every match tests them on—marksmanship, target transitions, movement, and gun handling. These fundamentals are combined in different ways and tested under pressure. Enough is happening in practical shooting to obfuscate how much the basic tools drive your success or failure. There are various challenges, such as moving targets, close targets, far targets, partial targets, running, shooting while moving, and so on. On the face of it, USPSA is infinitely diverse and very complex. The fact is that winning comes down to building the best set of tools that will work for all the jobs you have to do.

CHAPTER 1
WHAT IT'S ALL ABOUT

I have been teaching Practical Shooting for more than a decade. Watching thousands of students fire millions of rounds over the years has taught me quite a lot about shooting. I kept seeing the same patterns repeated over and over again. I would see the same mistakes on the same types of drills. These mistakes were easy for me to see and understand because I was already an experienced shooter. To make a student understand them was not easy.

Over time, I started to modify drills or design new ones. This helped highlight the patterns of mistakes I kept seeing. What I found is that if a student could see and feel a mistake, then that was understanding. In many respects, to see and feel something is better than just the intellectual understanding of what is happening.

This process of studying patterns, refining drills, and testing in classes has led to a simple set of exercises that highlight the most common errors found in shooting. If these errors are seen and felt, then they are understood. These "ah-ha" moments lead to breakthroughs in people's shooting. For example, understanding that you are pushing the gun down during rapid fire and understanding how to fix that can jump you up to the next level of performance. Two months later, you will not be the same shooter.

CHAPTER 2
DIAGNOSTIC PROBLEM

It is my firm belief that more people would get better at shooting if they had a better understanding of the cause-effect relationship between what they are doing with their gun and where the shots end up on targets. I don't think many people understand why the shots end up where they do. In most cases, when engaging a target with two shots, most people couldn't look at the holes and tell you with any certainty which hole belongs to which shot.

There really is a big disconnect between what happens and why it happens for many shooters. They view shooting as some sort of black box or voodoo magic. They input some ideas like "hold the gun really hard" and then see some output on the other side with very little understanding of what really happened.

The reason this is vitally important is if you have some clarity about what is happening and why it is happening, you are going to have better technique. You won't be able to help it. If you see that you are pushing shots off target, you will want to stop pushing them off target. It is as simple as that.

Connecting the dots between what happens and why it happens is complex, and that's the reason most people can't connect the result to the technique, and then don't understand what corrections to make.

The reason this book is structured this way is because it should help people connect those dots. The following diagram *(Figure 1–1)* is of a "regular" shooting scenario. Looking at where the holes are on target, it would be very difficult for even an expert shooter/instructor to offer clear insight.

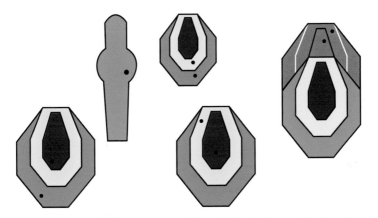

Figure 1-1: The diagnostic problem—What is happening here?

Errors are typically broken into a few categories, such as marksmanship fundamentals, transitions, movement, and gun handling (draw, reload, etc.). The approach taken here is to isolate each category of errors into a simple drill or set of drills. This then controls for other errors and eliminates them as a possible cause of bad shots. This will help you narrow down on your specific faults as a shooter and eliminate those faults.

In a sense, the goal here is to minimize the diagnostic problem. What is happening and why it is happening will become much clearer if you understand the ideas in this book *(Figure 1–2)*.

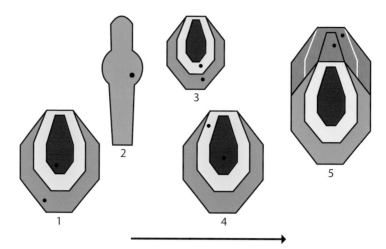

Figure 1-2: The diagnostic problem answered—Answers come by understanding technique and order of engagement.

1. Second shot pushed low
2. Good shot
3. Aimed wrong spot
4. Dragged on transition
5. Over-transitioning

CHAPTER 3

PURPOSEFUL PRACTICE

Due to how errors are found, this book is broken down into two main sections. The first section is the marksmanship section, which goes over the basic skills you need to fire a pistol while standing in one spot and have the bullet strike that target to the point you are aiming on each trigger pull. The next section moves into skills that are needed to become a more effective shooter in the action shooting disciplines. The section will focus in on problems that are induced when movement and other skills are introduced into the equation.

As we move into the third part, which focuses on drills, it is essential to point out that the focus on each drill that needs to be paid close attention to along with what the acceptable target hits look like. You can go through thousands of bullets merely going through the motions on a drill and will not experience any improvement in overcoming your issues and most likely become even more frustrated with your performance.

It is also important to point out that as you assess, diagnose, and fix one main issue you might be having, you will find another underlying minor issue come to the surface. Reference the diagrams used throughout this book to reassess your marksmanship and practical shooting skills as they develop, evolve, and improve.

NOTE: The acceptable target hits and diagnostic diagrams in this book are written from the perspective of a right-handed shooter. A left-handed shooter should mirror the diagram with the explanation to diagnose the root cause of their issues (Figure 1–3).

A)   B)

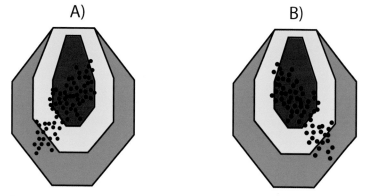

Figure 1-3: How to mirror for a left-handed shooter—The A) target shows the results of a right-handed shooter on a double drill. The B) target shows how the results would look for a left-handed shooter. BOTH shooters should both apply the advice of less firing hand grip.

PART 2
MARKSMANSHIP

CHAPTER 4
THE FIRST FUNDAMENTAL

The first, most important, and hardest fundamental to learn is marksmanship. It has been said, many times, that there are two parts to action shooting. There is the visible part: the running around, reloading, stage strategy, and all that associated stuff, and then there is the noisy part. Marksmanship is the noisy part. No matter what anyone tells you, your success in shooting is driven in large part by your marksmanship ability. The running around and all that other stuff is window dressing in many respects to the visible part.

A mishmash of interrelated concepts drives the noisy part of shooting. I want to briefly discuss each of these things and then demonstrate how they are linked together. After that, we will go over each of these things in detail, and then I will provide some drills you can do at home and at the range in order to improve upon your shooting and master these marksmanship concepts.

CHAPTER 5

GRIP

The first principle is the grip. This is essentially how you interface with your gun in order to hit the targets. Grip isn't just how you hold your pistol; it is also how you manage your pistol during the recoil, after the shot goes off. A proper grip is very challenging to learn because of the recoil control element. Every time you pull the trigger, you are likely changing pressures in your hands. This means that you might have an idea for what you want your grip to be and you can perform that technique on demand in sterile conditions (no time limit, non-competition, etc.). But when you are actually shooting "for real," the pressure in your hands is continually shifting to compensate for the recoil, and your proper grip will feel like a moving target.

To complicate matters further, your grip on your pistol will be very difficult to assess or even be aware of because you are constantly going to have the gun recoiling in your hand. It becomes very difficult indeed to figure out what is happening because as you are trying to grip the gun properly, the blast and recoil keep confusing the situation. It is hard to know your grip pressure when the gun keeps moving around.

The question you probably have right now is, "How should I hold my gun then?"

The main thing I want to propose is that this is mainly a hand pressure consideration and much less a matter of hand placement. For most readers of this book, it isn't their first exposure to material on how to hold a handgun (if it is, you may want to consider reading *Practical Pistol Reloaded* prior to this book). The firing hand goes high up into the beavertail and wraps around the gun. The support hand wraps around the grip frame, high up. Some people like to wrap their fingers up the trigger guard, while others use the trigger guard as a stopping point.

The much more important question here is, "How hard should I hold the gun?"

I want to express a few ideas here that all seem contradictory:

1. Grip the gun as hard as you can without inducing trigger control errors or shaking.
2. Grip the gun as soft as you can with your firing hand.
3. Crush the gun with your support hand so hard that it is uncomfortable.

I am going to explain each one of these ideas in turn so that you get a full understanding of what hand pressure should be like.

1. Grip the gun as hard as you can without inducing trigger control errors or shaking.

Obviously, the more force you can apply to holding onto the gun, the less it is going to flip around in your hands. This means you want to grip the gun as hard as possible without introducing any problems. It is tough for most people to induce a substantial amount of shaking by over-gripping. It's possible; it just doesn't present that often for most shooters. If you are over-gripping, then obviously you should back off a little bit. The shaking can come from either hand.

The more common issue is gripping too hard with your firing hand that you sympathetically move the gun when you pull the trigger. For most shooters, this means they need to consciously put effort into **not** trying to grip the gun really hard with their firing hand in order to correct the issue.

2. Grip the gun as soft as you can with your firing hand.

If you understand the above idea about over-gripping with your firing hand causing sympathetic problems with trigger control, then you might start trying to consciously relax your firing hand a little bit. For many shooters, the way to make the idea stick is to have them relax their firing hand as much as they can force themselves too. In their mind, the firing hand will feel like they are barely hanging onto the gun. This usually isn't the case; they are just acclimated to a super hard grip with their firing hand.

Generally, people do their shooting and their recoil control with their firing hand, and the support hand just helps hold the gun up. In order to do firing with one hand and support with the other, it really feels like they are holding the gun super loose. Just remember when you are doing the experimentation that your perception often distorts reality. Check the video in addition to going with your feelings when you are working out your grip.

3. Crush the gun with your support hand so hard that it is uncomfortable.

It is one thing to say it should be uncomfortable to put proper pressure on the gun with your support hand. It is quite another thing to force yourself to actually do it. Commonly, the skin gets removed from my hands by the amount of pressure my support hand clamps down with. It takes conscious effort to force yourself to grip the gun properly and to regrip properly after reloads.

CHAPTER 6
INDEX: TRAIN TO BE A LASER

Constant work on marksmanship fundamentals is key to developing yourself into an effective competitive shooter. It is also the most beneficial use of your ammunition when you are doing live-fire training.

When the gun hits where you point it, irrespective of how aggressively you are shooting it or how much pressure you are under, then you will be able to work your way through a stage at the limit of how fast you can move from spot to spot or transition from target to target. Your dry-fire training on these facets of shooting will be simple to do and very effective.

I like to think that I am training to be able to point my gun around like it was a laser and put bullets anywhere I point. As soon as I get that part down, then the rest of the sport is just learning to point my gun from spot to spot. It all becomes effortless.

"Index" is your ability to grip your gun and point it where you want to. It is the way your stance and grip interface to allow you to aim the gun at things you want to aim at immediately. An index is something that will naturally develop as you train your draw into your grip and transition from target to target. The important idea to understand is that if you don't have the ability to look at a target and then draw your gun with the sights showing up in your vision aligned and ready to shoot, you will quickly develop that ability as you start your training. That ability will get much stronger over time as well.

CHAPTER 7
ACCEPTABLE SIGHT PICTURES

Once you become competent at shooting, you need to learn how to shoot faster. In many respects, shooting fast is just learning where you can cut corners. The area where many shooters fail to cut corners is on learning what they can get away with in terms of sight pictures. The "traditional" sight picture of "equal height, equal light" or "hard front sight focus" is simply not needed for most of the targets you deal with in a real practical shooting match *(Figure 2–1)*. Once you accept this idea, I recommend you start experimenting with different sight pictures in order to see what works for you.

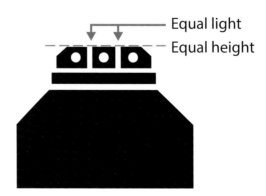

Figure 2-1: "Traditional" sight picture with equal height/ light between the front and rear sights.

Here are some possible sight pictures you might try with iron sights:

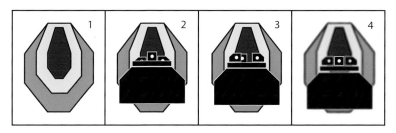

Figure 2-2 Examples of the sight position listed below.

1. Look at the target, with no tactile or visual confirmation of sights. Think about holding your gun over a wall or some similar scenario where you cannot see the sights and target at the same time.
2. Front sight visible on target. The rear sight not used.
3. Front sight visible through the rear notch. The front sight position could be anywhere in the notch.
4. Front sight aligned in the center of the notch centered on a target area.

Another point to consider here is whether you should put your eye focus on the target or the front sight of the gun. Most people prefer to bring their focus onto the front sight when the shots are perceived as difficult. This means they will know the exact position of the front sight for those shots and they feel more comfortable aiming.

Personally, I prefer to just look at the target all the time, and my sights always appear as blurry. This is a simpler system, but it does require quite a bit of training to shoot with confidence in this way.

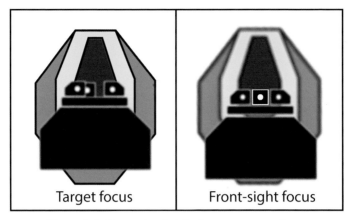

Figure 2-3: Example of sight focus vs. target focus.

With Dots, the list might look like this:

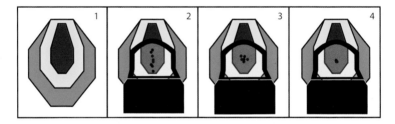

Figure 2-4: Examples of sight position listed below.

1. Look at the target, no tactile or visual confirmation of sights. Think about holding your gun over a wall or some similar scenario where you cannot see the sights and target at the same time.
2. Dot on the target in the aiming area. It isn't stable and may appear as a streak.
3. Dot wobbling in the aiming zone. The dot isn't entirely stable but is staying in the aiming zone.
4. Dot stopped and stable. Not perceptibly moving.

With dots, you should always look at the target and not attempt to focus on the dot.

I think most shooters can academically understand the concepts of different sight pictures for different targets and distances. The problematic part is the implementation. You need to have your skills to the point where you truly approach targets differently on a subconscious level. The discipline to wait for everything to line up for a harder shot while simultaneously smashing close-range targets with virtually no confirmation of your sights is not an easy thing to do and does require practice. This is an area where I frequently make corrections in classes.

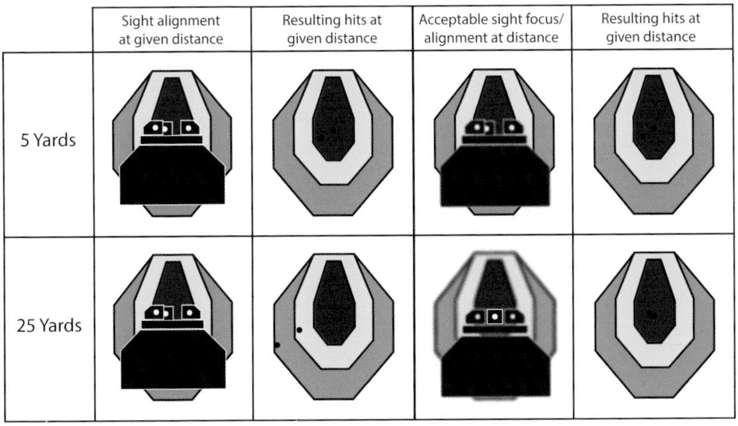

	Sight alignment at given distance	Resulting hits at given distance	Acceptable sight focus/ alignment at distance	Resulting hits at given distance
5 Yards				
25 Yards				

Figure 2-5: Example of how the same sight picture will change hits at distance.

CHAPTER 8
RESPECT THE TARGETS

A big part of competitive shooting is learning what you can get away with for certain targets. You don't very often need to do "traditional" marksmanship stuff perfectly. When you don't need "perfect" trigger control or a "perfect" sight picture, then it is a completely unproductive use of your time to do those things. Aiming more, aiming better, however you want to think about it, doesn't really help on the close and midrange targets.

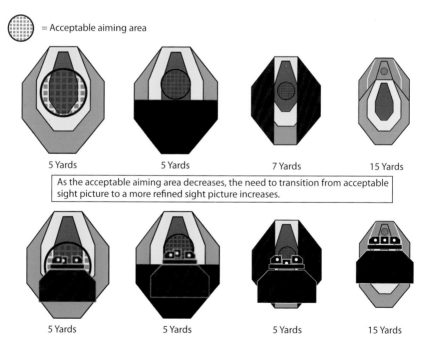

= Acceptable aiming area

5 Yards   5 Yards   7 Yards   15 Yards

As the acceptable aiming area decreases, the need to transition from acceptable sight picture to a more refined sight picture increases.

5 Yards   5 Yards   5 Yards   15 Yards

Figure 2-6: "Respect the target."

As much time as you spend learning what you can get away with, you do need to keep in mind that you can't take any targets for granted *(Figure 2–6)*. You can never disrespect a target. An "easy" target that you don't do the right things on can still be a missed target very easily. Learn what you can get away with, but never disrespect targets. It will bite you.

CHAPTER 9
SHOT CALLING

"Shot calling" is the concept of knowing where your shots are going as you fire them. This concept is absolutely critical to develop if you wish to compete at a high level.

The most common expression to explain shot calling is "see your sights lift." The idea here is that you see your sight lift out of the notch as recoil starts to happen. The last position of the front sight you saw before it started rising in recoil should be where the bullet is headed.

I think this concept of shot calling is a bit limited in terms of how you are going to be gathering information about where your shots go. I use the physical sensation of the gun in my hand (did I move it?), dirt puffs behind targets, blurring of my fiber optic, and more in order to have a better understanding of where my shots are going as I fire them.

Shot calling is a lot like trigger control. It is a nebulous concept in many respects that you develop over time with lots of effort but never will really master. The thing you should focus on for purposes of your training is that the better you get at calling shots, the better you will get at everything else. When you transition on to a target and start shooting too early, you will immediately recognize your mistake. When your gun is bouncing around as you are shooting while moving and you put a shot down too low, you will know why. Shot calling unlocks your ability to learn.

I think of shot calling as "knowing what is happening" when I am shooting. It is how you link the cause (your shooting) with the effect (where the bullets go). You will learn everything about shooting as you develop your shot calling.

CHAPTER 10
TRIGGER CONTROL

Trigger control is the ability to fire a shot without moving the gun away from the point of aim. Like aiming, the definition of "acceptable" changes as the target difficulty changes. At close range, you are able to mash the trigger back almost carelessly, and the gun will remain on target. At long range, you will need to hold the gun like a vise and carefully press the trigger straight back so that absolutely everything remains perfectly still, except for your trigger finger.

The main problems with developing good trigger control are speed and recoil.

It is common for shooters to have solid trigger control when they aren't shooting a live gun. However, add in ammunition, and the recoil moves the gun around so much that they can't really feel or see the gun moving sideways as they pull the trigger. I really think the only solution for this is to change your focus from sight alignment to your hands to overcome the problem. That is simple to write, but complex to actually do. To pull the trigger straight back, you need to change your focus from the sights, the noise/blast, and all other distractions when shooting a live gun and instead focus on holding your hands still and just moving the trigger finger. It isn't easy!

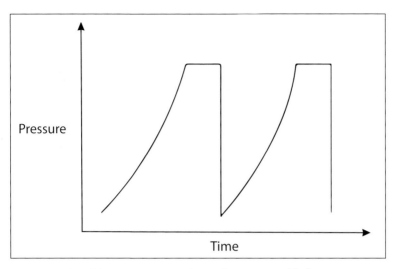

Figure 2-7: Trigger pressure—Smooth pressure added to trigger.

The other common problem with trigger control is the speed issue. It is one thing to hold the gun still and pull the trigger slowly *(Figure 2–7)*. It is quite another to hold the gun still and pull the trigger quickly. It is another level still to pull the trigger straight, but as fast as you can and still be applying smooth pressure to the trigger *(Figure 2–8)*. The natural human tendency is to slow down when making mistakes. You won't really develop proper trigger control by going that route.

Be very careful about aiming the gun and then abruptly smashing the trigger *(Figure 2–9)*. This is a common mistake when people encounter difficult shooting. You must understand that aiming more/better isn't usually the hard part. The difficulty will come from accepting that you need to smoothly apply pressure onto the trigger without moving the sights. That simply will not happen by aiming a lot, then bashing the trigger.

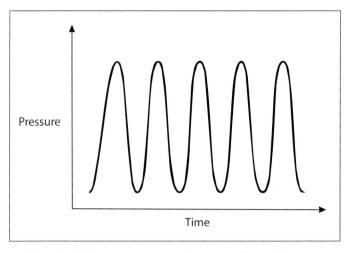

Figure 2-8: Trigger pressure—Compressed smooth trigger.

The number one thing you need to bring to the table to get solid trigger control is self-awareness. I have seen it in every case; as soon as someone becomes aware of which muscles in their hands or arms are moving the gun off target as they try to shoot, they correct the issue almost on their own. Instead of focusing on the result (hits on target), pay attention to your body and how you influence the gun. You need to learn to hold the gun still!

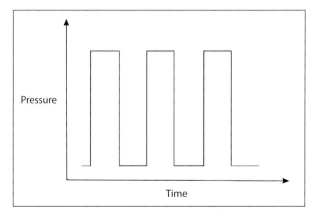

Figure 2-9: Trigger pressure—"Binary switch."

CHAPTER 11
RECOIL MANAGEMENT

A frequent question that arises during the discussion of grip will be the idea of recoil control or recoil management. How should one handle the recoil from their gun? It is frequently the case that people will make problems for themselves by working far too hard to stop the gun from recoiling.

The fact is, you can't really do very much about recoil. Hold the gun hard, so it doesn't move around inside your grip. Let the gun recoil without trying to hold the gun perfectly flat. You only need to push the gun down to the extent it pushes you up. If you are holding the gun hard, it doesn't push up that hard.

You can test how much the gun pushes up on you by doing something called the "Measurement Drill" (developed by Hwansik Kim). Try holding the gun loosely and not trying to return the gun to your original aimpoint at all. Just fire a round into the center of a target and let the gun recoil up without fighting it. Look at where the gun ends up. On a 7-yard target, if I hold my gun loosely and let it recoil up, it will change the point of impact about 6 inches. It doesn't take much force for me to push the gun down enough to counter the upward force.

What I look for when watching a student shoot is that their hands and gun all move together as a unit. Their

Hwansik Kim—IPSC and USPSA Shooter.

support hand and firing hand should be locked on the gun, and every piece (each hand and the gun) moves together. Usually, people's support hands keep coming off the gun or their firing hand torques on the gun in some ways. Those things shouldn't be happening.

I should also point out that you aren't going to accomplish much in the way of control by using your upper body or your back muscles. You just can't make the gun shoot appreciably "flatter" by using lots of your muscles on it, and using lots of upper body muscle in the attempt to control your gun will not have good effects on target transitions. It is challenging to transition your gun around precisely when your upper body is tense.

CHAPTER 12
ONE-HANDED SHOOTING

One of the more common challenges that make people uncomfortable is shooting one-handed. This might be strong hand only or weak hand only, but the basic technique is going to be the same regardless of which hand you are using.

The most obvious issue is the lack of a support hand or a "control" hand clamping onto the gun and keeping it from flipping around in recoil. This means you need to do the firing and the control all with one hand. The most common problem this creates is causing shooters to push down into the gun and send shots low. Since any pushing for speed causes problems, the natural defense mechanism that shooters have is to "slow down and get their hits."

The way to shoot one-handed is to grip as hard as you can without causing "shaking" in your sight picture as you aim at targets. I would recommend gripping right up to that point. This will minimize the "flip" that your gun will inevitably have. It is crucial to understand that the gun *will* flip around more when shooting one-handed. It will be awkward and uncomfortable. It can feel almost out of control if you are only used to shooting with both hands. It will require practice to get used to the feeling of your gun's recoil impulse with one-handed shooting. Don't make any mistake about that.

There are a few other changes you should consider when shooting one-handed:

Instead of standing squarely facing the targets, think about blading your firing side towards the targets some more. This will better align your body, so you have a good range of motion when shooting only one-handed. Targets directly in front of you aren't quite as comfortable as being bladed when shooting one-handed.

You should also think about what to do with your non-shooting hand. Pulling it into your body so that it isn't swinging around at your side is comfortable for most people. If the stage requires you to hold something in your hand, then this may not be an option for you.

I would recommend staying away from bending your elbow to bring your gun in closer to your face. This makes it quite a bit harder to aim with iron sights, due to a reduced distance from your eye to the front sight. It isn't damaging with dot sights, however.

I would also be mindful about your point of aim vs. point of impact. Many people prefer to cant the gun slightly when shooting weak-handed. This tilts the sight more towards the dominant eye, sure, but it also can alter the point of impact when shooting at an extended range. You should understand these issues and be mindful of them.

In any event, the main problem of shooting one-handed is going to be pushing into the gun to fight recoil and, in turn, throwing your shots low. The standard defense mechanism of "slowing down" will protect your ego at low-level matches, but it will not really solve the problem. When shooting one-handed, you must focus on your firing hand, hold it still, and press the trigger straight. There is no other way to do it.

PART 3
PRACTICAL MARKSMANSHIP

CHAPTER 13
GUN HANDLING

Gun handling (or "gun manipulation," if you prefer) is the catch-all term for anything you are doing to get the gun into your hands, pointed at the targets, and full of ammunition so that you can shoot. Drawing the gun out of the holster and reloading are typical examples. Picking up a gun from a table, loading a gun from empty, and fixing some sort of jam is a less common example, but it still happens.

In my view, your training of gun handling should be to facilitate actually shooting well. This means your draws and reloads should be subconscious and slick. You should be able to do these things in all situations without needing to think about it. The other, less common, actions should at least be consistently performed with very little thought required.

Obviously, the best place to practice these actions is at home during some dry-fire practice. Practicing drawing and reloading at home is a common thing for shooters to do. I believe most readers of this book have already done it, but I do have some specific advice to make your practice more effective and useful.

The number-one thing you absolutely must do when practicing fast gun manipulations is to "keep it real" regarding your grip on the gun. In other areas of this book, there was a discussion about the specifics of hand pressures and hand positioning on the gun. If you put any time at all into actually trying out the associated drills, then you will see that your grip being "close" isn't close enough. It needs to be perfect each and every time. The main problem with dry-fire practice is the lack of feedback. You aren't going to be seeing holes appear in targets (at least I should hope not) when working with an unloaded gun. You will not have the sensation of recoil pulling the gun out of your hands if your grip isn't right.

The lack of feedback means that you MUST pay meticulous attention to not just the speed you produce, but also the quality of your technique. Is your grip correct? Are you holding the gun tightly enough? Are you over-tensed on your shoulders? Every detail should be accurate, but it won't be without your constant attention. Many shooters can produce fast times in dry-fire by slopping their way through exercises, but then they don't get the same result when shooting live ammunition. It is their care and attention during dry-fire practice that is to blame for this. You don't want this to be you.

CHAPTER 14
DRAW

Many people believe your draw isn't really that important in terms of your performance in a match. In a 30-round stage, the difference between a 1.2-second draw and a 0.9-second draw doesn't seem like that much time. I believe this thinking is flawed.

Your draw speed correlates strongly with other skills. In order to draw and shoot a target, you look at the target and then drive your gun to that target. This is essentially the same skillset you use when transitioning from one target to another. In my view, bringing your draw speed and consistency up will help drive related skills to another level. All top shooters can draw and shoot very quickly, but what propels them to their level is their ability to do it consistently.

The starting point for developing a good draw is to understand your grip. Really understanding how to grip your pistol is not easy, and your ideas will change and be refined over time. So, I suppose a realistic starting point is to have at least an idea about what you want your grip to be. You draw into your grip after all, and you should have something in mind that will be your completed draw.

Once you know where you are going, you should start thinking about how to get there. In my view, a straightforward process for drawing your gun is going to make things easier. If you are trained in a 4- or 5-count (step) draw, I will discard that right away for competitive shooting. Instead of that, you should focus on two steps.

Step 1: Get your hands to the gun
Step 2: Get the gun pointed at the target with a proper grip

That's it, 2 steps.

In the first step, you bring your firing hand on to the gun. Ideally, your holster allows you to get a firing grip on your gun. That means it is off your body enough. You can wrap your thumb around your gun and hold the gun essentially the same way you would if you were shooting. If you are shooting a carry holster for IDPA or something like that, it may be a problem. But do the best you can, given the equipment you have to work with.

Your support hand should come over near your holster. You don't want to endanger yourself by putting your support hand in the path of the muzzle, so you don't get in front of the gun, but over towards the gun so you can start gripping the gun as soon as it comes out of the holster.

In step 2, you aggressively snap the gun up out of the holster and get a grip on the gun with your support hand as you bring the gun up to your eye line. Ideally, the grip is complete before you can even see the sights on the target.

There are some important ideas I want to address that happen during step 2. Firstly, you should do no extra gun movement when the gun comes up. Very commonly, people throw the gun (almost) up to the target, and the movement of the gun is very imprecise. Almost invariably, the gun needs to be brought back down to the target because it went up too high in the first place. It is common to see the first shot in a fast shooting sequence go high because the shooter is pushing to get the first shot off quickly *(figure 3–1)*. You must be aware of this issue during your training and not "overdraw" the gun. Bring it to your eye, and that's it.

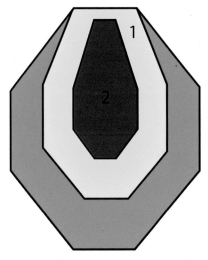

Figure 3-1: Draw—Throw gun at target, and first shot is off. Correction is to relax shoulders.

Along those same lines, try to avoid extraneous movement in your body. As you push to go fast, things will tend not entirely to be perfect, but try not to crouch down as you draw. Try not to twist your hips excessively. Try to be very stable aside from the required movement of your arms. This isn't easy to do, but it is something you will want to check in a video. Look for signs that you are compressing your body during your draw stroke and attempt to avoid it.

One other thing I would avoid is starting to "prep" the trigger during step 2. This is very common for people to do and it seems logical. You will be shooting very soon after drawing, so you may as well get the trigger ready to go. This is especially attractive with Double Action triggers that require quite a lot of pressure to set off. In my view, prepping the trigger early doesn't result in faster times, but is definitely a more complicated technique. I have seen this technique make life difficult for people more often than not.

Regarding training, you can train step 1 and step 2 easily at home. Push yourself to go fast, but try not to tense up parts of your body that don't need to be. You hold the gun primarily with your hands. There is no reason to tense up your entire body just because you are holding a gun.

Using your timer with the par setting, you should be able to get a grip on your gun in 0.4 seconds. This is from hands at sides. With your hands in some other position, it will likely cost about 0.1 seconds in order to get a grip on the gun. So, if you are starting with your wrists above shoulders, it might be 0.5 seconds to grip your gun in the holster and move your support hand near the holster.

To draw the gun and point it at the target, I think 0.7 seconds is pretty good with a production-style holster onto a simulated 7-yard target. If your hands are not starting hands at sides, then add a tenth of a second to that. As the simulated ranges extend, then it will add time for you to find a precise sight picture (remember, your acceptable sight picture will vary based off the distance). By the time you are working on a 25-yard target, getting an A zone sight picture and proper grip in one second flat is extremely fast.

Please note, these times are for sight pictures without pressing the trigger. I think when you are training for a

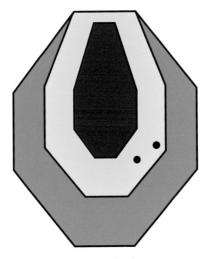

Figure 3-2: Draw—Aim/looking at wrong spot.

fast draw, always incorporating a trigger press is not a good idea. You might well develop the habit of pressing the trigger quickly without really confirming the sight picture. This is a common problem.

You should obviously train different start positions and target configurations. But a good goal is to be able to look to a spot and drive the gun aggressively onto that spot with your eyes and have your grip be perfect. It isn't an easy thing to do, but it will push your shooting to the next level.

CHAPTER 15
RELOAD

Reloading quickly and reliably is obviously something you need to learn to do. In the low capacity divisions, you will reload (often more than once) on almost every single stage of a USPSA match. You will often be moving and sometimes moving in awkward directions. It isn't an easy thing to do to be moving backward to your non-dominant side and need to reload at the same time. It takes practice to be able to execute these skills. It will require even more training to be able to perform these skills in a high-pressure match environment subconsciously.

In terms of technique, it is relatively simple. Hit the magazine release button with your dominant hand (twisting the gun around in your hand to reach the magazine release is totally fine) as you go for a fresh magazine with your support hand. Index the magazine in your support hand and bring it up to the gun. Seat the new magazine in the gun. Once the magazine is seated, then regrip the gun and carry on with shooting the course of fire.

The main technical points you should consider are the exact position of the gun as you reload, the way you grip the magazines, and the regripping process on your gun. I will handle each of these points in turn.

First, the way you position the gun as you reload is the single most crucial factor that will make things fast and consistent. Generally speaking, the higher up you hold the gun, the faster you can be (at least in theory), and the lower you hold your gun and closer to your body it is, the more reliable and consistent things are. I think the best thing for most people is to bring the gun down to about chest level. If you are using a gun with a considerable magwell, you may opt to hold the gun higher up. I wouldn't go as low as belly button level in any situation.

The way you angle the gun is significant as well. You should point the magwell towards the magazine pouches. Generally, shooters point the magwell out away from their body, even though the magazine will be coming off the equipment on their body. This causes extraneous movement to become a necessary movement as they bring the magazine around to where the magwell is located. Avoid this step and position your gun, so you don't need to contort the magazines at all.

A good test for the gun position is to stand with your hands empty and then quickly grab a magazine out of the pouch. Bring the magazine up to chest level quickly. Your gun should be matching this natural orientation of your magazine.

When I grip the magazines, there are a few rules I follow:

I grip the magazines with the base pad firmly in my hand. I then lay my finger on the front of the magazines (the part with the bullet tips facing it. It doesn't matter so much if your mag pouches are bullets forward or bullets out, the grip on the magazines should be the same).

Always grip the magazines the same way, even when you aren't reloading on the clock. Even during administrative handling of my gun, I grip the magazines the same. This acclimates me to always have good control over their position.

When seating the magazine in the gun, you want to trust yourself to be able to seat the magazine in one motion. If there is any equipment issue like magazine spring tension or base pad length, you absolutely need to address it during your dry-fire training. It absolutely should be reliably handled in *one* motion.

Finally, when you regrip your gun, it should mirror the end of your draw stroke. The grip should be back on the gun and ready to go. I know a lot of people like to do fast reloads for Instagram and they don't worry about a good grip when they are jamming up a 0.8 reload. But for real matches, you need to have a grip you can actually work with. Do not neglect to regrip your gun correctly!

In terms of training, there are a few exercises I really like and recommend.

You can train the reloads in isolation by starting with your gun pointed at a target. Just practice ejecting a magazine and bringing a fresh one up to the magwell. You don't even need to insert the new magazine. Just get it to the gun! After you learn your magazine release and are sure you are ejecting magazines, you actually don't need to start with a magazine in the gun. You can just hit the release and bring up a fresh mag. This can be done very quickly by people that train. Six-tenths of a second is a good time for it.

If you do a complete reload, mag out, mag in, and aimed at a simulated 7-yard target, then 1 second is very fast.

I also like to practice reloading as I move. Move in all directions around your dry-fire area, as fast as you can, and be able to reload smoothly as you move. Work all the way back in your pouches, so you get used to reaching for magazines if you had to do multiple reloads on a stage. All of these skills should be subconscious.

One final note about reloads is to be sure you occasionally practice how to reload a completely empty gun (not just from shooting, but also from a holster and from a table). Not all guns for IPSC/USPSA have a slide stop, so you may need to practice recognizing the gun is empty and racking a round in off a fresh magazine. If you have a slide stop, you should have a reliable technique for using it. I prefer to use my support hand thumb to hit my slide stop. This ensures I have seated a magazine in the gun before I hit the slide stop.

CHAPTER 16
TRANSITIONS

Transitioning from one target to the next is where most of the time between good shooters and world-class shooters is found. It makes sense; the time it takes to acquire a target and then shoot it is critical in a speed-shooting sport. This is likely obvious to an astute reader.

What might not be obvious is how you can develop world-class transitions of your own.

At its core, the process of a target transition is super simple. Your eyes find the target you want to shoot, your gun goes to the target, you then shoot the target. The complicated part of this is in doing it quickly and efficiently.

As shooters develop, they tend to quickly realize how essential target transitions are and then try to develop fast transitions of their own. The way they do this is to "go faster." They push the gun as aggressively as they can from target to target. They put as much muscle in the process as they can. They usually improve their times from the starting point and feel this is a successful strategy.

The problem with the "go faster" approach is that it is very imprecise and is counterproductive when you consider how accurate your transitions are. When you aggressively slam the gun from one target to the next, it is difficult to make that movement precise. You end up dropping points all over the place. A better way to go is to de-emphasize the physicality of the transition from one target to the next and instead focus on cutting down the lag time from one action to the next.

Let me break this down into steps:

1. Shooter realizes it's time to transition to the next target. (This is done by mentally "being done" with the target they are shooting or the action they are performing.)
2. Shooter acquires the next target in their vision as they move the gun towards the target.
3. The gun arrives at the next target.
4. When the shooter gets an appropriate sight picture, they start shooting.

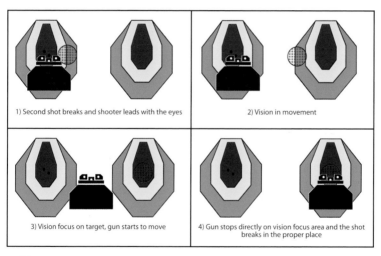

1) Second shot breaks and shooter leads with the eyes

2) Vision in movement

3) Vision focus on target, gun starts to move

4) Gun stops directly on vision focus area and the shot breaks in the proper place

= Vision Focus Area

Figure 3-3: Transitions the correct way—vision moves to exact point, then gun moves.

Typically, there are significant delays for most shooters between "getting done" on a target and getting their gun moving to the next target and "getting started" shooting on a target after their gun gets there. These delays tend to be to the tune of 0.1 or 0.2 seconds each time. This commonly adds up to 5 seconds or more a stage. A tenth of a second delay at the beginning and end of each target transition adds up FAST.

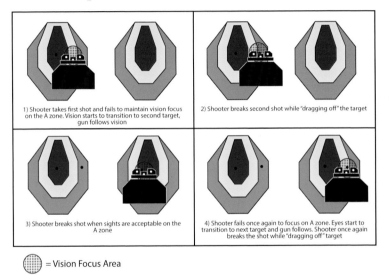

1) Shooter takes first shot and fails to maintain vision focus on the A zone. Vision starts to transition to second target, gun follows vision

2) Shooter breaks second shot while "dragging off" the target

3) Shooter breaks shot when sights are acceptable on the A zone

4) Shooter fails once again to focus on A zone. Eyes start to transition to next target and gun follows. Shooter once again breaks the shot while "dragging off" target

= Vision Focus Area

Figure 3-4: Transition wrong—gun moving with vision.

Instead of focusing on how quickly you get the gun from one target to the next, you should be focused on reducing delays and cutting out lag time. The gun should get moving to the next target immediately when you are "done" on a target. You need to start shooting as soon as the sights show up at your next target. You don't have a couple of tenths of a second to get tucked behind a comfortable sight picture. You need to start shooting as soon as you can.

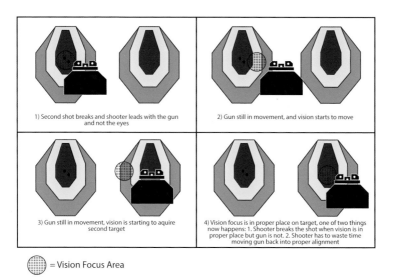

1) Second shot breaks and shooter leads with the gun and not the eyes

2) Gun still in movement, and vision starts to move

3) Gun still in movement, vision is starting to aquire second target

4) Vision focus is in proper place on target, one of two things now happens: 1. Shooter breaks the shot when vision is in proper place but gun is not. 2. Shooter has to waste time moving gun back into proper alignment

⊞ = Vision Focus Area

Figure 3-5: Transition wrong —dragging off target.

Of course, as you train to be right on the "razor's edge," you will occasionally get your wires crossed. Sometimes, you will not quite be done on a target when you start moving to the next target. Sometimes, you will start shooting before your sights show up on the next target. As long as you can recognize these errors at the time they occur, you aren't going to have any problems correcting them.

Another thing to consider is the precision of your target transitions. It is one thing to transition the gun to a target. It is another to transition the gun to an A zone. It is another thing still to transition the gun to a specific point that you want to hit. It really doesn't take appreciably more time to at least attack a specific aimpoint instead of attacking a whole target. You should program yourself to go precisely to the point you want to hit.

Concerning technique, two points absolutely cannot be overstated. The first is that your eyes lead the

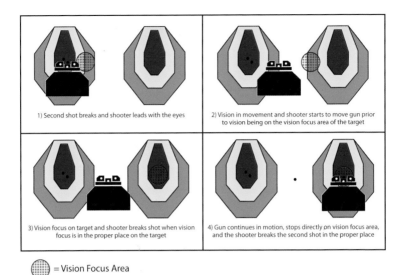

1) Second shot breaks and shooter leads with the eyes

2) Vision in movement and shooter starts to move gun prior to vision being on the vision focus area of the target

3) Vision focus on target and shooter breaks shot when vision focus is in the proper place on the target

4) Gun continues in motion, stops directly on vision focus area, and the shooter breaks the second shot in the proper place

= Vision Focus Area

Figure 3-6: Transition the wrong way—gun moves before vision is focused on target.

gun everywhere. Use your eyes the same way you drive a mouse pointer around on a computer. You look where you want to go, and almost by magic, the pointer will appear where you are looking. That sensation of effortless aiming is exactly the way you should be using your gun. You look at a target, and the sights will simply appear where you are looking.

The other important issue is that the main problem area if you are "muscling" the gun around and having it appear imprecisely for you, is shoulder tension. If you are trying to push the gun quickly from spot to spot, your shoulders will probably tense up. That will be a cue for you to consciously relax your shoulders and let your target acquisitions flow from your vision instead of trying to push the gun around fast. One of the most common mistakes to make when transitioning, especially when under match pressure, is to over-muscle the gun from one spot to the next. Ideally, you should move the gun from one aim-point to another aimpoint as fast as you can while having the gun stop smoothly and precisely.

If you see your sights move past the center of a target you are transitioning to, then that is an indication you are over-muscling the gun. Relax your shoulders a bit and de-emphasize transitioning the gun.

The primary way to train on better target transitions is to set up some targets in your dry-fire space and practice only the transition element. The way you set up the targets doesn't matter all that much, but if you have a good variety in terms of partial targets, full targets, and steel spread around (not evenly spaced), then you can quite quickly learn the basics.

I recommend establishing a par time to get a sight picture on each target and then working to reduce that par time as much as you can. It is essential to be very honest with yourself while you do this training. You need the time to come from getting the same sight picture faster, not from sweeping the gun through the targets without paying attention to the sight pictures properly. Basically, practice aiming your gun from spot to spot quickly. DO NOT worry about pulling the trigger when doing this training. You can work that element separately.

In certain situations, you do need to apply a bit of "muscle" to your target transitions. That situation occurs when the transitions get wide, or the targets start to get very close. If you are doing a 120-degree transition on 5-yard targets, then you might consider pushing the gun around more aggressively. A bit of dry-fire on the specific scenario can quickly show you how much muscle is productive. However, once again, if you see the gun go past your intended target area and then come back, you pushed the gun too hard, too far.

CHAPTER 17

MOVEMENT

Movement seems like a broad topic, but the reality is if you pay attention to a few basic principles, you are going to be able to move around pretty well.

The "rules" are as follows:

1. Be ready to shoot as you arrive in a shooting position.
2. Always strive to be ready to move.
3. When you move, move as aggressively as you can.

The rules are simple, but quite a lot follows from these few simple rules.

Rule number 1 is rule number 1 for a reason. It is the most important thing. When you get to a target, *be ready* to shoot it. It absolutely doesn't matter how fast you are at target engagement if you get started engaging a target later than your competitors. The name of the game is "shoot sooner, not faster" and it is absolutely critical for your development that you strive to be ready to shoot as soon as you are in position.

Readiness is a bit of a more complicated concept than it might seem. Obviously, you want the gun up in front of your face. You should be looking to get your sights on the first target you plan to shoot straight away. Most people understand that. What is a little bit less intuitive is just how early you can get your sights on a target. You don't even need to be able to see the target in order to start aiming at it (*Figure 3–7*). You know where it is, you know where it will appear, you should begin aiming at that spot, even if there is a wall in the way. One of the most common corrections I make in a class setting is getting people to start aiming sooner.

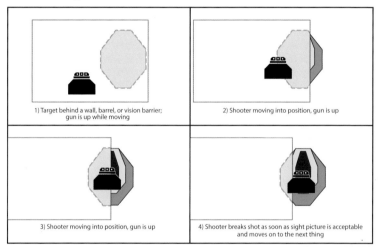

1) Target behind a wall, barrel, or vision barrier; gun is up while moving

2) Shooter moving into position, gun is up

3) Shooter moving into position, gun is up

4) Shooter breaks shot as soon as sight picture is acceptable and moves on to the next thing

Figure 3-7—The "Correct" way to have the gun up coming into position.

You should also be considering your stance and shooting platform as you come into a shooting position. Your feet spread apart wide and knees bent is going to help you be ready to shoot. The sooner your sights are stabilized on the target, then the sooner you can start shooting! If your sights are bouncing around as you come into position, the solution is almost always going to be found by sorting out your lower body. Set your feet into position gently, so your sights remain stable. Use your knees as shock absorbers, so you remain ready as you settle down.

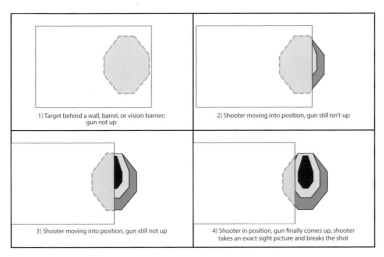

Figure 3-8: The wrong way to come into position.

The second rule also seems simple, but it is another thing that is so commonly corrected in a class setting that it's hard to believe. Try to be ready to move to the next position as you set up in a shooting position. Setting your feet on the ground with your weight evenly distributed and your knees bent will absolutely facilitate more aggressive movement to the next place you need to go. Commonly, shooters like to put all their weight on one leg or stand up straight and tall. The best habit is that of always striving to be set up low and wide and aggressive. Be ready to move to the next place!

This brings us to rule number 3. Run as fast as you can. This also seems so obvious and so simple that you wouldn't think it needs to be mentioned, but it does. The fact is, most shooters are not going all out on a stage when they move around. Only a few shooters really give it everything they have when they are on a stage. Be one of the shooters that is going 100 percent. By going all out, every time you move, you will also learn to get yourself slowed down, low and stabilized as you come into a position from a full run. If you don't ever properly develop your brakes, then you will just never be able to use all your horsepower to motor around the stages effectively.

The ideal training for movement from one spot to another is dry-firing. You don't need a whole lot of live shooting to train to move around the stage. You do need to do a whole lot of proper practice with an unloaded gun. This is a similar style of training to the transition training I recommend. Work on moving yourself quickly to the next firing position and practice slowing yourself down so you can effectively start laying shots on target.

It is critical to understand that your main focus as a competitive shooter is to stop smoothly and efficiently as you come into position. Remember, shoot sooner, not faster. What helps you shoot sooner is to start to brake as you come into position. The same as you gently work your brakes as you roll up to a stop sign in your car, you need to massage your brakes as you stop yourself moving into position on a stage. You aren't ready to shoot if you are sliding on the range surface or bouncing around. Get yourself stopped smoothly and maintain stability. When you arrive in the next shooting position, you will be ready to smash alphas.

CHAPTER 18
SHOOTING ON THE MOVE

Shooting while moving is an important skill to master in order to start cutting time off in between shooting positions and possibly even eliminating shooting positions. If you carefully watch top level shooters work their way through a stage, you may see quite a few situations where they don't stop moving as they shoot through a stage. The ability and confidence to shoot and move at the same time is something that needs to be developed with quite a lot of training.

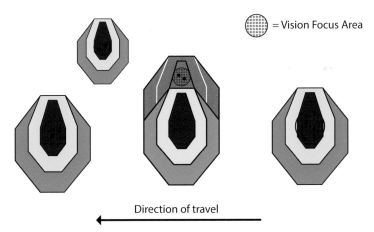

= Vision Focus Area

Direction of travel

Figure 3-9: Shooting on the move correctly—looking at center of target and actively aiming while moving.

The technical aspect of shooting while moving isn't very complicated. Bend your knees a bit more than usual and use them as shock absorbers as you move. So long as the sights are more or less stable as you move around, you should be able to shoot effectively.

One thing that is important to try is shooting with a target focus. Instead of the conventional "hard front sight" focus where the front sight appears clear, and the target appears blurry, try looking at the target and having the sight picture appear blurry. In my experience, the lack of sight clarity will mean you don't perceive every little bounce in your sight picture. This can help reduce hesitation with your shooting.

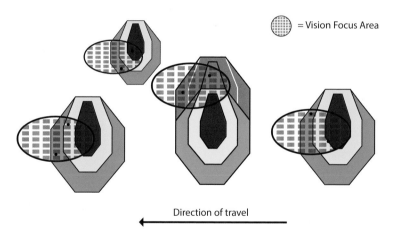

= Vision Focus Area

Direction of travel

Figure 3-10: Shooting on the move wrong—vision travels with movement and not actively aiming.

The other advantage to target focused shooting while you move is that it helps mitigate a common error. It is normal that people will fail to "actively aim" as they shoot while they move (*Figure 3-9*). This is to say that they will aim for an instant and then start shooting without adjusting that aim. This means that as they shoot their target, their aim point will drift off the target as they move (*Figure 3–10*). By looking at the target, your gun will naturally drift towards where you are looking. This is the same fundamental situation as looking where you want to transition the gun to.

Shooting while moving can essentially be trained the same as target transitions. You draw your gun and move as you transition the gun through a set of targets. The important thing to point out here is that you have one more metric to pay attention to in addition to speed and accuracy. The distance you move during the drill (movement speed) is essential. Taking baby steps as you shoot isn't very productive. Being able to engage targets at a fast walk effectively is a great place to be.

CHAPTER 19
STAGE PLANNING

One of the most attractive parts of Practical Shooting as a sport is that generally, you aren't going to shoot the same stage twice. This keeps things fresh and makes every match a new challenge.

The downside is that it is challenging for new shooters to learn how to approach stages because they are always different and always changing. I have a simple set of guidelines people can use to come up with a plan for stages. Before I get into the specifics of how to break down stages, there is an essential point to address. It might actually be the most important idea when it comes to stage breakdown.

Execution is king; planning is secondary. What this means is that shooting well and executing your stage plan well is what matters. Having the "best" plan is unlikely to offer you a significant advantage. If you are running stages 5 or 10 seconds slower than the top guys at your club, you aren't going to gain it in the stage breakdown section. It just isn't going to happen. However, if you are indecisive and unable to settle on a plan, then you will have a severe disadvantage. Having a plan that you are firm on is *far* better than waffling between plans or focusing on minutia.

With all of those things out of the way, I have a simple 5-step system that I have been using and teaching for quite a while.

1. Assess stage requirements
2. Pick your path
3. Look at options
4. Decide on options
5. Check for risk

1. Step one is to assess the stage requirements. How many rounds is it? Where do you need to go in order to see all the targets? Are there any positions that provide only one chance at a target array (a must hit position)? These are the sorts of big-picture questions you want to answer early. Don't walk through the stage counting out shots and figuring out where you will reload. *Do* figure out where all the targets are and where you need to go.

2. Pick your path through the stage. Generally, a right-handed shooter will work uprange to downrange, left to right. That isn't always an option. You should figure out a plan that facilitates natural movement and minimizes how far you have to move. If you are unsure between two paths, pace out the steps and see if one offers an advantage over the other path.

3 & 4. After picking your path through the stage, you should examine the smaller choices you have available to you. Consider the possible reload points (given the round count, etc.). Should you shoot a set of targets left to right or right to left? Should you shoot a particular target as you move or not?

This is where you need to call on your training and experience to make choices that will work for you. Would you rather shoot near to far or the reverse? Only you can answer those sorts of questions. If you have any doubt, just shoot targets in the order you see them and be done with it. Don't think about it too hard because execution is always king.

5. As a final step, think about your plan's risk level. Is there someplace in the stage where you are likely to have a problem? Maybe you are shooting a 10-round division, and you are planning on 9 small pieces of steel on the same magazine. Does that feel risky to you? Is there a way to mitigate that risk without causing any other problems? These are things to think about if you want to change your plan.

Now you might have noticed that you have a firm plan going into a stage; however, something goes awry, you need a couple of extra shots on steel, you take a make-up shot you were not planning to, and suddenly you find yourself lost, can't remember how many rounds you have where the next target is. At this point, you can either continue with catastrophic thinking or calm down and get yourself back on course. Reload as soon as you need to, and then reload once again where you planned to in your original plan and get yourself back onto your stage plan and simply continue to execute. It is quicker to take a couple of shots off an unplanned magazine and reload where you planned to continue firing "subconsciously," than it is to turn a stage into a math problem and figure out new places to reload.

PART 4
DRILLS

CHAPTER 20
DRAW–DRY/LIVE FIRE

Exercise for: The draw exercise is used to learn how to grip your pistol quickly and consistently, then rapidly get your pistol to your index in order to engage targets.

Setup notes:
All you need for this drill is a single target. For dry-fire, feel free to use a miniature target scaled to the proper distance.

Procedure:
Start in any desired start position (hands at sides facing the target is normal). At the tone, draw your gun, grip it properly, and aim it at the target. When doing dry-fire, don't press the trigger. Just disengage gun safeties (if you have them) and get a firing grip. Work to reduce the par time.

When testing your draw speed using live ammunition, fire any desired number of shots into the target. The time you should carefully assess is the first shot time. Firing multiple shots instead of just one shot will help you assess the quality of your grip on the gun.

Focus:
Focus on quickly establishing a proper firing grip on your gun and getting the gun on target quickly.

Goal:

Getting a consistent and safe first shot off in 1 second at 7 yards with live ammo is an excellent goal. At 15 yards, 1.2 seconds is quite good.

When doing dry-fire, achieving a sight picture on the target from hands at sides at 7 yards in 0.7 seconds is quite good. At 15 yards, getting a sight picture in one second or less is very good.

Changing start position or extending the range further will, of course, add a bit of time to the draw.

In any event, the times listed above (with A zone hits consistently) are very good for competition.

Commentary:

Your draw speed and consistency is very important for competitive shooting. You quite simply must be fast at looking to a spot, gripping your gun properly, and bringing your gun to that spot. Many people believe their draw speed is not terribly important for competition. In a sense, that may be true. A first shot speed a tenth of a second one way or the other doesn't matter too much. However, the speed with which you can present the gun is interrelated with target acquisition and transition speed. Developing your draw will help you shoot whole stages faster, even if the actual draw speed doesn't affect things a whole lot.

I recommend that for dry-fire training, you mostly stay away from pulling the trigger. It is very easy to race the second beep (the par time) with the click of pressing the trigger instead of racing up to a sight picture on the target. You do not want to be in the habit of pulling the trigger without a sight picture, and if you aren't careful, you can induce the habit by incorrect dry-fire.

Another concept to think about is the ability to effectively draw in any conceivable situation. Most of your time measurement can be done in the "standard" positions, but be sure to practice turning to face targets or standing up and drawing from a seated position or really any variation you can think of. That flexibility will serve you well in your competition.

Dry-Fire Tracking:

Draw at: 7 yards
PAR TIME: Sight picture in 0.7 (from hands at sides)

Date:	Draw Time:	Met par?	Proper Grip?	Notes

Draw at: 15 yards
PAR TIME: Sight picture in 0.9

Date:	Draw Time:	Met par?	Proper Grip?	Notes

Draw at: 25 yards
PAR TIME: Sight picture in 1.1

Date:	Draw Time:	Met par?	Proper Grip?	Notes

CHAPTER 21

RELOADS–DRY-FIRE

Exercise for: Learning to reload fast and consistently.

Setup notes:
You just need a single target. Set it about 7 yards away.

Procedure:
Start with a proper grip on your pistol and point it at the center of your target. At the tone, drop the magazine and replace it with a fresh one from your belt.

Focus:
Your grip on your pistol should be as close to perfect as you can get it after you finish a reload. This is the most important part of this drill.

Goal:
Being able to reload in about 1 second is quite good. If you account for reaction time to the beep, this makes a goal time of 1.2 seconds quite good.

Commentary:
Expect to spend a good deal of your time learning how to reload fast and efficiently. Basically, you need to stand in place and get very comfortable changing magazines. It

needs to be able to happen without a whole lot of conscious thought on your end. It just needs to happen without any drama.

There are a few things you can do to facilitate easier training.

Once you confirm that you are doing a good job getting the old magazine out of the gun, then you don't necessarily need to drop a magazine every time. It will save you from needing to pick the old one up off the floor. Just be sure you occasionally check to make sure you are still hitting the magazine release properly.

You should also be paying attention to any "missed" reloads. Are you making the same mistake every time? Is there some pattern to the problems you are seeing? A small change in where you hold your gun as you reload or how you grasp the magazines can make a huge difference. Pay attention to what's happening and don't be shy about changing things, if you must.

Reload Tracking:

Single Reload: Single magazine change
PAR TIME: Sight picture in 1.2 seconds (no trigger squeeze)

Date:	Met par?	Acceptable Sight Picture?	Proper Grip?	Notes

Triple Reloads: Change magazines 3 times back to back.
PAR TIME: Sight picture after last reload 3.5 seconds

Date:	Met par?	Acceptable Sight Picture?	Proper Grip?	Notes

CHAPTER 22
PRACTICAL ACCURACY

Exercise for: Learning the proper grip and trigger control skills needed for shooting tight or difficult shots at realistic match pace.

Setup notes:
For this drill, you need to make the target an A zone only. You should paint around the A zone using black (hardcover paint). Another option is to cut the A zone out of the target and turn it around, so you have an A zone surrounded by white, creating a no-shoot all the way around the A zone.

Procedure:
Pick a distance to shoot from. A good place to start is at 10 yards. At the start signal, engage the target with six rounds. Strive to shoot as tight a group as possible in the center of the target. There is no specific time limit for this drill, but you are required to press the trigger again as soon as your sight returns from recoil and stabilizes in the center of the A zone. Shoot six strings from your chosen distance, a total of 36 rounds, then assess the target.

Focus:
As you shoot this drill, your mental focus should be on your hands and hand pressures. You should not be

mentally focused on the sight alignment piece of shooting. That part should be allowed to work on autopilot.

Goal:
Learn to shoot the gun fast and straight to an acceptable standard for competitive shooting. All A zone hits at 20 yards is very good for deliberately paced shooting in this drill.

Commentary:
Practical Accuracy is used to learn your grip and trigger control in the context of shooting at a deliberate shooting pace. This doesn't mean you shoot slowly; it means you see your sight return for every shot and that's it. This should be a reasonable simulation of shooting tight shots under a bit of match pressure. When you see the sight where you want it, you typically will want to press the trigger really quickly in a match setting. This drill will help you identify and correct common issues associated with that.

The basic idea here is, you are going to aim at the exact center of the A zone and do your best to lay shots on top of each other. Given the fact that you will be shooting immediately when you see the sights where you want them, you aren't going to be shooting perfectly centered groups all that easily. As the distance increases, it will become challenging just to hit the A zone.

The most important thing to emphasize here is that this drill is just designed to create circumstances for you to learn your grip and fundamentals. That's all. Learn to shoot the gun quickly as straight as you can shoot it. You do this by paying attention to the feel in your hands and trigger finger and by relentlessly trying to make things better and better.

It is important to point out that your assessment of the target is going to be compromised if you try to nail down a draw at your maximum speed. Make sure your grip is right, and the sights are aligned before you start shooting. Going the maximum speed on the draw isn't really the point here.

Assessment:

Targets should appear as follows:

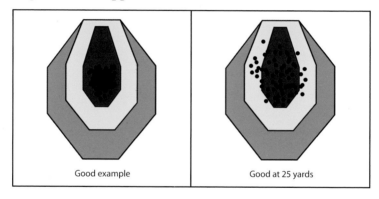

Good example   Good at 25 yards

Incorrect Targets and possible issues:

What went wrong and how to fix it:

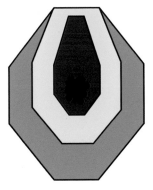

This target looks excellent at first glance, but ask yourself if you were indeed shooting as soon as the sight returned to the target. Could you shoot more aggressively? There shouldn't be any delay or lag time between the sight coming back to your aim point and the next shot being fired.

What went wrong and how to fix it:

This is a very common problem. The shooter is pushing the shots low by pressing the trigger sideways or pushing into the expected recoil. Holding the gun more softly with your firing hand will help relieve sympathetically moving the whole hand along with the trigger finger. Hold your firing hand still as you shoot, and this problem will be mitigated.

What went wrong and how to fix it:

The gun is not returning to the center of the target before the next shot is fired. The most usual cause is insufficient support hand pressure on the gun in order to keep it "flatter." Shooting more slowly is your last resort to fix this problem.

What went wrong and how to fix it:

Sometimes shots are pulled right. This can be due to hooking the trigger finger around the trigger and pulling it sideways or breaking your wrist as you pull the trigger. Pay attention to the feel of the gun in your hands in order to identify your own specific problem.

CHAPTER 23
DOUBLES DRILL

Exercise for: Doubles is used to learn the fundamentals of grip and trigger control while shooting rapid fire.

Setup notes:
All you need for this drill is a single target.

Procedure:
Start at your desired distance with hands relaxed at sides. At the signal, draw and get a sight picture on the target. When you have your sight picture, fire a pair of shots at your predetermined pace (details below). Stabilize the gun on target again, get a sight picture, and then fire another pair at the same predetermined pace. Repeat this process until you have fired a total of four pairs (eight rounds). Fire six strings at the target for a total of 48 rounds, then assess the target and score it. Work at any desired distance.

It is important that you pause your shooting in between pairs of shots. The attempt here is to simulate transitioning to a new target.

Focus:
Focus on your grip and trigger control.

Goal:

The goal is to learn to shoot the gun very quickly and have shots land in a predictable pattern centered in the center of your target. You can then adjust the pace of your shooting, so it gives you desirable results at any distance.

Guidelines for pace and accuracy with iron sights:

5 yards	MAX	100% Alpha
10 yards	.20 split	95% Alpha
15 yards	.25 split	90% Alpha
20 yards	.30 split	85% Alpha
25 yards	.35 split	80% Alpha

Guidelines for pace and accuracy with dot sights:

5 yards	MAX	100% Alpha
10 yards	MAX	95% Alpha
15 yards	.22 split	90% Alpha
20 yards	.25 split	85% Alpha
25 yards	.30 split	80% Alpha

Commentary:

This drill is the brother drill of "Practical Accuracy." Instead of shooting at a deliberate pace where you see the sights realign before you trigger the next shot, you will be shooting rapid fire pairs (similar to what you do in a match) and learning to grip the gun properly and control it through that experience.

A perfect place to start is the 5-yard line and pulling the trigger on each pair as fast as you possibly can. This will give you a proper understanding of what you are trying to accomplish.

One of the ideas that many people have trouble with here is the idea that you aren't going to wait to see your sights return before you fire the second shot in a given pair. In most cases, you will be shooting faster than you can consciously react. This is a normal situation for a match, of course, but for some reason in the context of trying to hit the center of a target, people don't like shooting that aggressively. Just understand that the pace of your shooting is predetermined and you need to figure out your grip and trigger control in order to get the result you want. Shooting slowly and getting hits you like doesn't fix anything. Just be aware that when you look at the above goal chart, you need to make the speed part happen first and the hits part will be a byproduct of sorting your grip out.

Another thing to pay attention to is when you get "trigger freeze." If you are unable to reset the trigger during high-speed shooting, your firing hand is too tense, and you need to relax it some. There is no real alternative about that.

The last caution I have for you here is to make sure that you are shooting pairs of shots. Don't shoot a long string of shots. That isn't the idea here, and it will end up being a lot different. Also, you don't need to bring the gun down from the target between pairs. That may introduce aiming errors into the equation, and that wouldn't be helpful at all.

Assessment:

Targets should appear as follows:

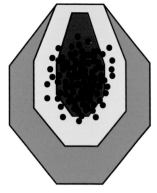

Good pattern speed up if possible.

25 yards—Some C zone hits acceptable.

Incorrect Targets and possible issues:

What went wrong and how to fix it:

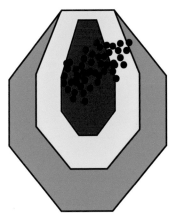

With shots going high, you either need to slow down or grip the gun harder with your support hand. Review the goal guidelines and get an idea about what you should be able to expect. In most cases, just grip harder and learn to hold the gun flat.

What went wrong and how to fix it:

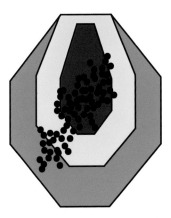

This is a common issue. Relaxing your firing hand a bit will help you stop sympathetically pushing into the expected recoil before the gun fires. Pay attention to your firing hand and hold it as still as you can as you shoot.

CHAPTER 24
BILL DRILL

Exercise for: The bill drill helps test your draw speed and grip quality in the same drill. You need to be able to get a proper grip, but very quickly.

Setup notes:
This drill is done with a single target at 7 yards.

Procedure:
Draw and engage the target with 6 rounds. The normal time limit for all A zone hits is 2 seconds.

Focus:
Focus on getting your grip together quickly.

Commentary:
Once you get your grip sorted out on drills like "Doubles," and you have developed a pretty quick draw, then the "bill drill" is a great way to test yourself. A competent shooter should be able to draw the gun quickly and get 6 rounds into an A zone in 2 seconds or less. Some shooters can go quite a bit faster than that!

The main thing to do when shooting this drill is to pay attention to what is happening with your body. The stress from the tight time limit might force some mistakes you haven't made before.

It is common to push so hard on the draw that the gun goes over the top of the target and comes back down into the A zone. You also might be "death gripping" your pistol with your firing hand as you draw it. This will cause trigger freeze. You need to be paying attention to how your body feels as you draw your gun or it is going to be challenging to get the results you are looking for.

The bottom line is that the "bill drill" is a test you need to be able to pass with some degree of regularity if you ever want to be a top-level shooter.

Assessment:

Targets should appear as follows:

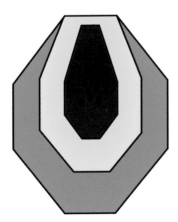

Incorrect Targets and possible issues:

What went wrong and how to fix it:

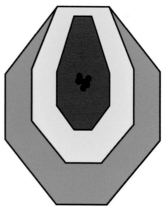

Shots are suspiciously close and tight. Ensure you are shooting at maximum speed and ensure you start shooting as soon as the sights get into the center of the target. If both those conditions are met, then this target is fine.

What went wrong and how to fix it:

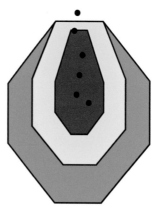

With insufficient support hand pressure on the gun, it will be easy for the gun to track up during recoil. Increase support hand pressure.

What went wrong and how to fix it:

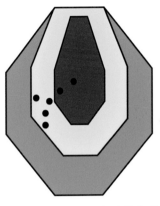

In a high-speed/high-tension drill like the bill drill, expect to over-tense your firing hand sometimes. That will push shots down left and low.

What went wrong and how to fix it:

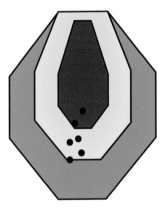

This distribution of holes is likely caused by too much firing hand pressure, which is causing the gun to sympathetically be pressed down.

What went wrong and how to fix it:

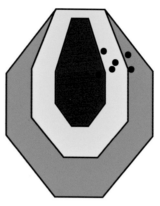

A tight pattern of shots in the wrong spot is indicative of aiming at the wrong spot. Make sure you look to the center of the target as you draw your pistol.

CHAPTER 25
TRANSITION DRILL

Exercise for: Understanding target transition basics.

Focus:
Pay attention to your eye and gun position as you start to push to engage the targets quickly.

Setup notes:
Set up a few targets. Feel free to use Steel targets and partial targets as desired. Close or mid-range is better than long range as the marksmanship fundamentals will be less important.

Procedure:
At the tone, engage all the targets at your match pace. If the results are consistently good, then push a bit faster. Keeping the same order of engagement allows for easier target assessment.

Commentary:
Target transitions are obviously an essential skill for you to understand. What should be happening is that you are able to shoot at the pace of your eyes, no faster and no slower. I recommend dry repetition (where you just practice aiming the gun quickly without pulling the trigger) as

well as live-fire repetition. If you are just a little bit faster than you are comfortable, then it will be a good "training zone" for you to see some mistakes and correct them.

Watch out for leaving the target too early with your eyes, getting on the trigger too early as you come into a target, aiming too much at a target that doesn't need it, and looking in the wrong spot on the target (causing hits in that spot).

During dry training, you should practice this drill without touching the trigger. You don't need to simulate shooting (not even a pause on target to fire shots in your head), just aiming quickly. Establish a par time and work to aim the gun at each target in turn as quickly as possible. Be sensitive to over transitioning. This will be apparent by the sights moving past a target, and then coming back to the center of the target. The solution is to remove unnecessary tension and try not to muscle the gun around quite as hard. The precision of movement will be faster than raw muscle every time.

You hit where you look; it is as simple as that. With some training, you can take charge of where you are looking and when you look there. This will make you shoot at the pace of your vision, which is as fast as anyone can go.

Assessment:

Targets should appear as follows:

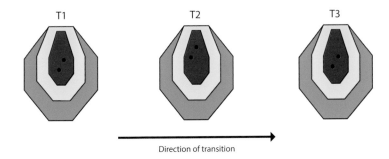

Incorrect Targets and possible issues:

What went wrong and how to fix it:

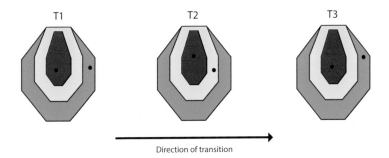

In this situation, the shooter moved their gun off the target too soon. Keeping your eye on the target until the instant you have fired your second shot is going to help with this.

What went wrong and how to fix it:

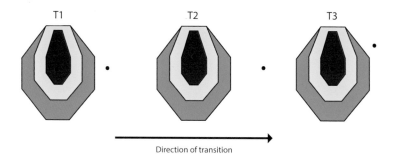

This is the same situation as above, just worse.

What went wrong and how to fix it:

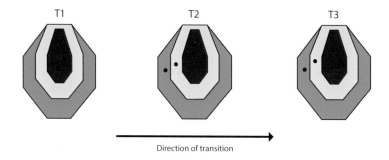

This pattern looks like the shooter isn't finding the center of the target with their eyes. The shots are hitting near each other, but often in the wrong spot. Find the center of the target with your eyes in order to fix this.

What went wrong and how to fix it:

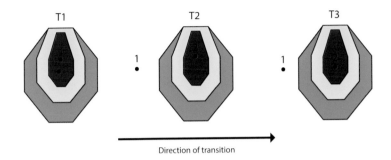

Direction of transition

In this case, the shooter is getting onto the trigger before the gun gets on target. This is common on close ranged target or when the shooter is rushing. It is vital to ensure you do not shoot until the gun gets to your desired aimpoint.

CHAPTER 26
DISTANCE CHANGE-UP

Exercise for: This drill is used to master switching between targets of different distance/difficulty smoothly and efficiently.

Setup notes:
Use 2 targets close (at 5 yards) and a single partial target or headbox set in the middle at 15 yards.

Procedure:
At the start signal, engage each target with 2 rounds. Be sure to do different target orders. Left to right, right to left, center target first, and center target last are all good options. Being able to shoot all the targets in under 3 seconds regardless of order is a pretty good pace.

Commentary:
Distance change-ups are a good workout for your target transition skills. The main idea here is that you should be able to very smoothly and immediately transition from target to target with no hesitation. You also should have a good idea about what proper shooting looks like, both on close-range high-speed shooting and on the more deliberate shooting you will do on the partial target.

"Distance Change-up" is a very challenging drill to do quickly primarily because of all the tension that will creep into your draw, your shoulders, your firing hand, and more. If you are able to overcome the tension that will come into your body as you try to shoot this aggressively, then you will be rewarded with being able to attack targets at exactly the speed of your sights. I can assure you that it will be plenty fast.

Assessment:

Targets should appear as follows:

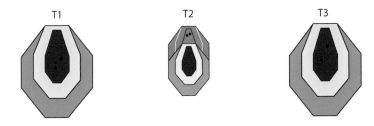

Incorrect Targets and possible issues:
What went wrong and how to fix it:

Low hits on middle target. Caused by pushing into the gun when the shooter perceives the shooting as difficult. Do not "pre-ignition push."

What went wrong and how to fix it:

T1   T2   T3

The fix is not to move your eyes until you are done shooting, and to wait until you see the sights where they should be before you start shooting. On the partial target, be sure to let your sights settle before you shoot.

What went wrong and how to fix it:

T1   T2   T3

Aim higher up on the partial target. Shots that are just clipping the no-shoot can sometimes be addressed by slightly adjusting your aimpoint and knowing exactly where your gun hits at various ranges.

CHAPTER 27
MOVEMENT

Exercise for: Learn the basics of movement in and out of position.

Setup notes:
Set up some targets you intend to shoot from one position and some targets to shoot from another. It is best to use a vision barrier to demarcate a shooting position. Typically, you want 5 or 6 steps between firing positions. As you develop, feel free to adjust that distance in order to emphasize different elements.

Procedure:
Engage the targets from one position then move to the second position and engage the appropriate targets from there.

Commentary:
This drill is where you work to apply the 3 rules of movement (discussed in detail elsewhere in the book) as best as you can.

1. Be ready to shoot as you arrive in a shooting position.
2. Always strive to be ready to move.
3. When you move, move as aggressively as you can.

These rules should be applied to your best ability at all times during your movement training. In addition to assessing the targets, it is extremely helpful to get a video of yourself or have a trained eye watching you.

Make sure your gun is up, coming into position. Make sure you set up wide. Make sure you move aggressively. If everything feels perfect to you, then go faster in order to find the weak points. This will end up being a constant process of training, assessment, and retraining.

Assessment:

Targets should appear as follows:

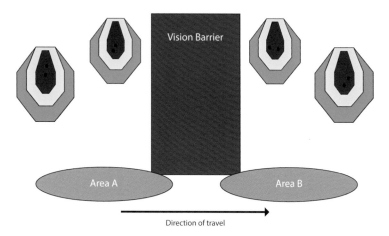

Targets should be hit with A's and close C's.

What went wrong and how to fix it:

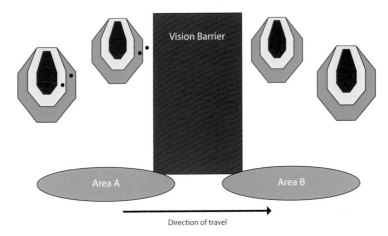

Make sure you are patient with your shooting before you move. The idea is to move aggressively, but shoot more comfortably. Shoot at your match pace. No faster and no slower.

What went wrong and how to fix it:

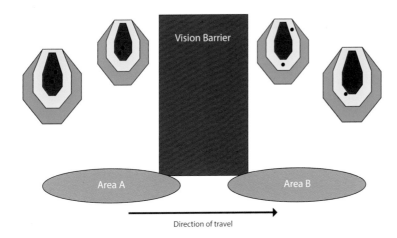

When you move from your first shooting area to your second, be careful to stabilize yourself. If your shots are dispersed vertically (as in this case), the likely cause is lack of stability. Bend your knees as you come into position and set your feet down gently.

What went wrong and how to fix it:

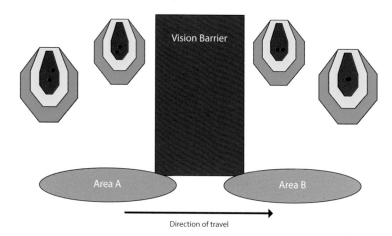

When you come into position and are shooting snake eyes, it is likely that you are not shooting soon/aggressively enough. You don't want to wait for a perfect sight picture before shooting; you want a "good enough" sight picture.

CHAPTER 28
SHOOTING ON THE MOVE

Exercise for: Refining your ability to shoot as you move.

Setup notes:
Set up some targets that you consider to be reasonable to shoot as you move. You need not make the targets extremely difficult or far. As your skills improve over time, do feel free to increase the difficulty of your targets.

Procedure:
Pick a start position and a movement direction. At the tone, move in your desired direction as you engage the targets. After engaging the last target, note your hits, time, and distance moved. The idea is to move as far and fast as possible while shooting reasonable points.

Commentary:
Learning to shoot while you move is a process that I think will take a bit of time, but it is well worth it. You will need to experiment with different movement directions and target difficulties, but in the end, you will have a good idea of what your capabilities are when it comes to match day. That's an excellent situation to be in.

The most important note I can give to any shooter is not to be afraid to "fail" when training on these things. I don't even really consider it to be a failure if you are unable to move and hit the targets accurately. You are learning your capabilities, and that's fine. You have the ability to improve over time, so don't worry if there is something you can't do.

Another thing to pay careful attention to is how fast you are able to move as you shoot. If you are only able to take slow baby steps because of the target difficulty, then usually you are better off just standing still and shooting. Again, don't feel like this is some kind of failure, just understand your capabilities and incorporate those concepts into your stage planning.

I strongly recommend shooting with a target focus as opposed to a sight focus when you are shooting on the move. I think it makes it easier to track the center of the target and keep your gun right where it needs to be on the target.

Assessment:

Targets should appear as follows:

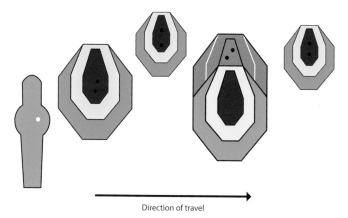

Direction of travel

Incorrect Targets and possible issues:

What went wrong and how to fix it:

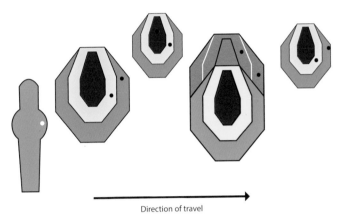

Direction of travel

In this situation, the shooter is aiming once and then shooting. The gun is moving off the target as the shooter moves. The solution is to keep refreshing your aim constantly. The easiest way to do that is to switch to target-focused shooting and look to the center of the target.

What went wrong and how to fix it:

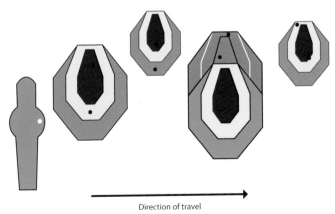

Direction of travel

Vertically dispersed hits are often caused by unstable or rough steps as you move. It is important to bend your knees and carefully step to ensure that your sight picture remains as stable as possible.

Glossary

"A" or Alpha: The maximum point scoring zone on an IPSC or USPSA cardboard target.

Dry-fire: Practicing with an unloaded firearm or dummy rounds.

Dot: The aiming point on an optic.

IDPA: The International Defensive Pistol Association.

IPSC: International Practical Shooting Confederation.

Live-fire: Firing the pistol with actual ammunition.

Rapid fire: Shooting at a competition pace.

Strong hand: Shooting with just your firing hand.

USPSA: The United States Practical Shooting Association.

Weak hand: Shooting with your support hand only.

ACKNOWLEDGMENTS

Many people have supported the creation of this work in one way or another: Jenny Cook did the majority of the actual work. Without her, this book wouldn't be a thing. Tim Meyers hassles me about deadlines and keeps me on task. Joel Park contributed the majority of the brainpower. Countless others helped me in some way . . . there are too many to mention.